Raising Lucy

Written and illustrated by
CAROL MUZIK

The True Story of Raising an Orphaned Wild Goose

Acknowledgments

Lucy – Live long, big goose
Nick – without you, there would be no story to tell
Joie Moring – for her love, support, guidance and design
Mom – for reminding us that dreams do come true
Lily and Humfrey – the two characters in our lives who still make us smile
Jennifer McCord and Roberta Trahan – for their enthusiasm and professional guidance
Jeff – for all the free meals during crunch time

Second Edition © 2011
First Edition and Text and Illustration © 2009 Carol Muzik
Published by Raising Lucy Studios LLC
Coeur d'Alene, ID USA
RaisingLucy.com
Printed in China
ISBN: 978-0-9820269-1-5

Book jacket author photo – Joie Moring

Publisher's Cataloging-in-Publication Data

Muzik, Carol.

Raising Lucy : the true story of raising an orphaned wild goose / written and illustrated by Carol Muzik. -- Coeur d'Alene, Idaho : Raising Lucy Studios, c2009.

p. ; cm.

ISBN: 978-0-9820269-1-5
Audience: ages 5-9.
Summary: What would you do if an orphaned day-old Canada gosling appeared on your doorstep? As weeks of caring turn to months, the little goose, Lucy, becomes part of the family, until her successful return to the wild.

1. Canada goose--Anecdotes--Juvenile literature. 2. Wildlife rescue--Anecdotes--Juvenile literature. 3. [Canada goose. 4. Wildlife rescue.] I. Title.

QL795.B57 M89 2009   2009932577
598.4/178--dc22   0909

On a sunny spring day in May on Lake Coeur d'Alene in Idaho, Nick was outside working in his yard. A man walked up carrying something very small.

"Hey, can you help me with this?" the man asked.
"Sure, " replied Nick. "What do you have there?"

The man handed him a tiny golden gosling. The gosling had wandered into the construction site where the man worked. It was all alone, and in the workman's way.

"I was on my way to the lake to set it free," the man explained.
"But I have to get back to work."

"We'll take care of it," Nick said, holding the little bird very carefully. Because of its black beak, black eyes, and black legs, Nick knew it was a baby Canada goose.

His wife, Carol, joined him in the yard. "Oh my! What happened to your parents?" she asked.

The gosling just looked up at them and peeped.

"We'll find your parents," they told the little goose, and promised that it would be very soon.

Canada geese flock together in the wetlands at the head of the bay, and Nick and Carol were sure they could find the little goose a home right away.

They got in their kayaks and began to search. The gosling hopped in the water and swam alongside. The baby paddled its little feet very hard, but it couldn't keep up and peeped unhappily.

"I think you need a rest," said Carol. She put the little bird on her kayak. As they glided along it walked around on top of the boat – watching the world zoom by.

In the wetlands, things were strangely quiet for a warm spring day. Nick and Carol looked and looked, but there wasn't a goose anywhere.

Sadly, they returned home with their orphan. "Maybe tomorrow we'll find your parents, little goose."

Lucy's wild and gentle spirit will always inspire my journey– may she also inspire yours.

Needing help and advice, Nick and Carol called the Fish and Game department. They were told that wild animals belong in the wild, so Nick and Carol decided they would just have to keep trying to find the baby goose a goose family.

They began a daily search for goose parents in their kayaks. As they looked around the bay, the little goose stayed very close.

In the wetlands, they found shy ducks and red-winged blackbirds calling to each other from the reeds. But there wasn't a single goose to be found.

Overhead, a hungry hawk soared. Though this was the gosling's true home, it was just too young to survive all alone.

And so, the gosling came home with Nick and Carol for one more day.

Days turned into a week – and they still hadn't found the gosling a family. The fast-growing goose was becoming a part of theirs, though.

The gosling followed them everywhere. During the day, they kept it outside with them – and in the evening, the gosling joined them in the house. Sometimes, they kept it in its big cage that Nick built. But often, the baby goose was free to wander around the house with everyone else.

Nick and Carol soon found out that you cannot house-train a goose – no matter how hard you try. So, they rolled up the rugs and laid towels everywhere on the floor. They hoped the goose would just stay *on* those towels.

The goose liked lying on the soft towels – it just didn't seem to know what to do with those fast-growing, long legs.

A couple of weeks passed. Nick and Carol didn't want to get too attached, and had been calling the gosling, Goose. After a while, though, that just sounded silly – so they decided she was a girl, and named her Lucy.

They still intended to return the baby goose to the wild, but they knew they'd done a lot of things wrong. For one thing, the family's black Lab, Lily, liked the goose. She always wanted to be next to Lucy – and Lucy liked being with Lily.

Lucy didn't seem to know if she was a dog or a person.
She certainly didn't know she was a goose. How
could a goose return to the wild if it was
friendly with animals and people?

How would Lucy know to stay away from danger?

Every day Nick and Carol took their 'family' to the lake. It was a sight to see them with their dogs and the goose. Walking together to their beach, Lucy and Lily often walked side by side.

Lucy would swing out her legs, running as hard as she could. She gave herself an extra boost by spreading her little wings to keep up. Like any other goose, she could hardly wait to get in the water.

Even though the whole family loved Lucy, Nick and Carol knew it was best for her to be with geese. They tried every day to find a wild goose family for Lucy, but the geese would just ignore her and swim on by. It was *so* frustrating!

Lucy loved the water and she was a very good swimmer. She swam deep under the surface like a loon, then she'd burst up with a big splash.

Running across the water, she flapped her wings hard on the surface. Splashing water everywhere, she turned circles in her own waves. Suddenly, she would dive under the water again – then, twenty feet away she'd pop to the surface like a cork.

Even though it seemed like Lucy was playing, she was also practicing skills she could use to survive and avoid danger in the wild. Lucy was learning how to be a goose!

A month passed, and Lucy was growing fast. She spent a lot of time grooming and preening—constantly nibbling at her feathers. Big gray feathers replaced her golden down, and her wings were taking shape. Her neck was growing long and strong.

She was also becoming tall and lanky. Lucy was getting so strong that she could now leap out of the water and onto their dock.

Nick and Carol called this her "teenage stage". She still made peeping sounds but she was losing the cuteness of being a fluffy yellow gosling. She wasn't little anymore—but she wasn't big enough to fly.

Lucy was growing so fast, and Nick and Carol realized it would soon be time for Lucy to be on her own.

Nick and Carol continued to take their family to their beach every day. They wanted Lucy to spend as much time in the lake as possible. While they walked, Lucy ran. She kicked her feet up high and ran as fast as she could. Sometimes she ran ahead of everyone else. She was funny to watch as she high-speed waddled towards the water.

If a goose could smile, Lucy definitely did.

She was quicker and more relaxed in the lake than she was on land. Swift and alert in the water, she knew the lake was her true home.

Nick and Carol enjoyed watching Lucy grow up.

A goose in the wild is in the water much of the time. In the wild though, a gosling would have the protection of watchful parents.

Lucy was still too young to be in the lake without Nick and Carol nearby, but they just couldn't spend all day at the beach. So, when Lucy was almost a month and a half old – they bought her a pool.

Lucy had a great view from Nick's and Carol's big deck. Birds and bugs flew by as she enjoyed the cool water. She cocked her head – swimming in circles to watch her flying friends.

Geese have amazing eyesight. Lucy was aware of everything—from the tiniest bug to the highest flying plane. She didn't miss a thing, and she saw it *way* before anyone else.

At just over a month and a half old, Lucy was beginning to look like an adult Canada goose. Black and white markings were coming in on her head and neck. Still, a telltale tuft of golden down sat on top of her head. It looked like a princess crown or a Mohawk hairdo, and it was a reminder that Lucy was still young.

Her wing feathers were getting longer. To clean them, she flapped and flopped them in the water, splashing water everywhere. Lucy was beginning to understand how her wings worked. She wasn't quite ready to fly—but she would be soon.

Like any other goose, Lucy took short naps throughout the day. And like all geese, she had excellent balance. She could sleep while standing on one foot. Sometimes, she'd even tuck her head onto her back or under her wing while snoozing.

When Lucy's eyes were closed she could fool an intruder. Her white eyelids made it look like she was wide awake. Now and then, it was important for her to check on things. So, still relaxed, Lucy would open one eye and scan the area. Bugs and birds flew here and there – but everything was calm. Then she'd close her eye to enjoy the rest of her nap.

Lucy needed to stay alert in the wild because of the animals that could hurt her – or worse, and her awareness of everything going on nearby showed that she was growing wiser every day.

One warm summer evening, Carol discovered Lucy in the side yard. It was dark, but she could see that Lucy was nose to nose with something *big*—like a raccoon.

A raccoon will kill a goose, so Carol quickly ran over – clapping and yelling to chase it off. But it slowly waddled away and climbed a nearby apple tree for cover.

Nick came out to look. "I don't think that was a raccoon."

Together, they walked over and looked up into the tree. There in the moonlight was a big porcupine clinging to the branches. Nick and Carol backed away, because a porcupine will use its quills to defend itself. But they mostly eat leaves and bark so it probably wouldn't have hurt Lucy. They worried, though, that Lucy was too quick to make friends, and wasn't ready to survive in the wild.

By the time Lucy was two months old, she had grown into a beautiful young-adult Canada goose. She was enjoying the feel of her big wings.

Standing tall in the water, she paddled her webbed feet and flapped her wings. Water flew everywhere and waves and bubbles swirled all around her.

As they watched, Nick and Carol wondered if it was time for Lucy to fly. But the question was – how do you teach a goose to fly? Since Lucy didn't have goose parents to teach her, they realized it might be up to them.

Remembering how Lucy followed them every day in the kayaks, Nick and Carol thought, maybe she would follow them around the lake in their ski boat. In order to keep up, Lucy would have to try to fly. Nick and Carol thought this could be a good plan.

They took the ski boat out – going slowly at first. Their dogs, Humfrey and Lily, were in the boat watching Lucy.

Lucy was in the water far behind, paddling her feet trying to keep up. Nick sped up, and Lucy ran as hard as she could across the water. She flapped her wings as she ran, but still – she wasn't taking off. Nick sped up even more.

Faster and faster the boat went—20, 25, then up to 30 miles an hour. Lucy ran even harder trying to catch the boat. Then – it happened. Lucy's wings lifted her up and finally, she was in the air.

Nick and Carol watched and cheered—*Lucy was flying!*

Wild geese fly at least twice a day when they're training the younger geese. Nick and Carol watched them and decided to fly Lucy twice a day too – once in the morning and then again before sunset. This helped build up her strength because Canada geese need to be able to fly very long distances. Every day they made Lucy's flights a little longer. When fall came, she had to be ready to migrate with the wild geese.

Their dogs, Humfrey and Lily, enjoyed coming along on the daily flights. Lily often sat in the boat near Lucy watching her every move. The dogs seemed to know that this was something special. Nick and Carol agreed—*everything* about Lucy was special! Still, they wanted her to be able to join the wild geese, and soon—it would be time for Lucy to leave.

Lucy liked eating grass and dandelions, along with fresh corn on the cob that Nick and Carol gave her every day. She also liked to search for food in the water near the beach. When she dipped her head underwater to nibble on plants her tail stuck straight up in the air.

Humfrey and Lily liked joining her for a swim and would fetch their ball in the water nearby. As Carol threw the ball one day, it landed too close to Lucy for Humfrey's comfort. Lucy had her head underwater, but he remembered when she bit him hard, and he didn't want that to happen again! Staring at the ball, Humfrey inched towards it. Lucy popped up for air and looked around. Humfrey stood very still until she dipped back under the surface. That's when he saw his big chance. He inched his way closer, until finally, he grabbed the ball – without a bite from Lucy!

Nick and Carol laughed at their funny little family. They loved having Lucy with them, but fall was coming. How much longer would she stay?

One early morning in late August, Lucy was flying near the left side of the boat. To avoid the shore, Carol had to turn the boat towards Lucy. With her wings spread, Lucy glided to the right – flying in front of the boat's windshield. All of a sudden, Lucy planted both feet on the windshield as the boat continued to zoom along. Carol wasn't sure what to do.

Lucy seemed fine so Carol kept going. Lucy kept her wings out, but she didn't flap them as she stood on the windshield. The boat flew through the water. Lucy stayed there, head pointing into the wind – like a giant hood ornament. Then – without any trouble – she gently pushed off and glided over to the right side of the boat.

Lucy was becoming stronger and more confident discovering new ways to take off and land. Nick and Carol laughed as they sped on their way. Lucy seemed more independent every day!

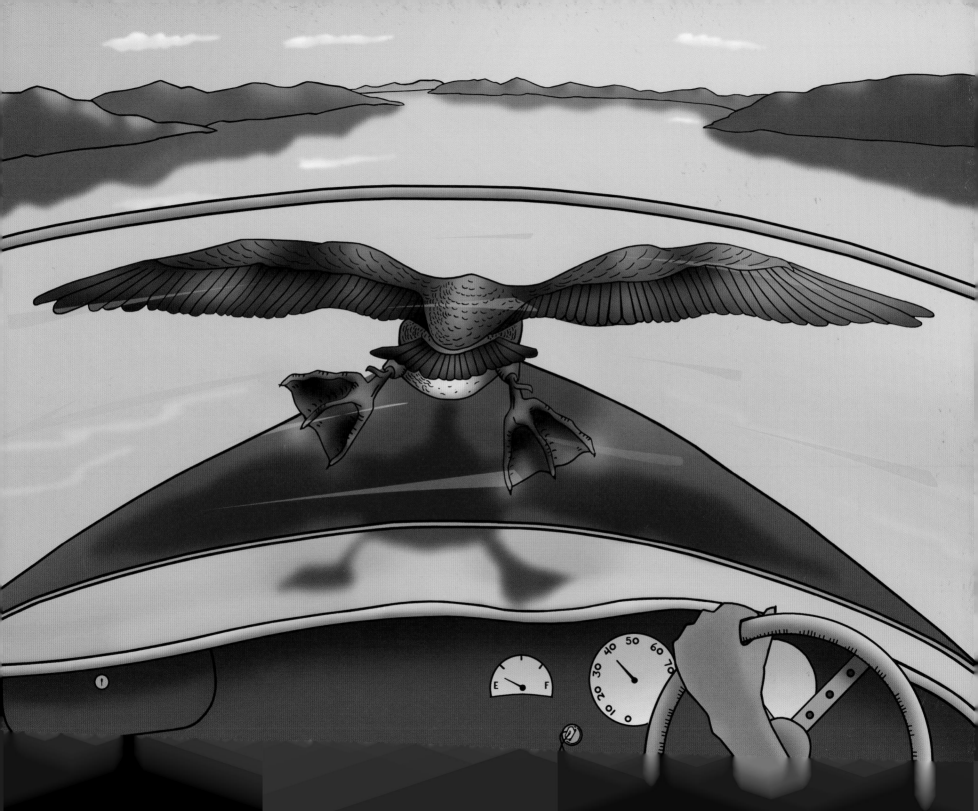

By the middle of October Lucy was five months old. She hadn't migrated with the wild geese, and Nick and Carol wondered if she ever would. Lucy had a family—Nick and Carol and their dogs—and she was still uncomfortable with her own kind.

It was getting colder and many of Lucy's summer bird friends were flying south for the winter. Some geese, ducks, coots, and wild turkeys stayed behind, but Lucy was shy and especially didn't care for the turkeys in the yard. The older Tom turkeys were bigger than she was, and came close to check her out. Lucy wasn't interested in being friends with turkeys, so she'd give them a sideways look and slowly step away.

She watched as the wild geese flew in formation overhead. She honked at them and they honked back at her, but still, Lucy wouldn't join them.

On a cold December day, a large flock of Canada geese flew in to see Lucy. Lucy joined them and they honked at each other and played in the water. She seemed to fit right in – in spite of living with people and dogs.

Nick and Carol hid quietly watching Lucy with her new friends. If Lucy saw them, she would make a big ruckus wanting to be with them. That would upset the wild geese, and they'd leave her behind as they flew to another part of the bay. So, Nick and Carol peeked through bushes to keep an eye on Lucy.

For several months Lucy spent most of her time with the wild geese. She even found a mate. Nick and Carol could only hope for the best as Lucy and the flock were gone for hours and days at a time. It seemed like she was happy living in the wild.

In early March, Lucy and her friends flew off, but they did not return. In spite of their worries, Nick and Carol knew that everything they wanted for Lucy was finally happening.

A whole year came and went without a sign of Lucy. What had become of their beloved goose? Nick and Carol thought about Lucy every day, but it was out of their hands now. They had to trust that they'd done some things right. Lucy was in the wild—right where she was supposed to be.

One early spring evening, Nick was on the dock tending to the boat. Suddenly, he heard a lone goose honking. It honked and honked and flew right over his head three times before landing in the water nearby. Nick called for Carol, "It's Lucy! Lucy's here!" Carol ran as fast as she could to see their long lost goose. The goose swam back and forth, honking and honking, as if to tell a year's worth of stories.

They couldn't believe it, but there she was, safe and sound—exactly a year later! They had no idea where Lucy had been, but she had come back to show them that she was a wild goose.

Their baby goose was all grown up, almost two years old—living happily in the wild—her true home.

Test Yourself on Lucy Facts:

1. What month was it that Lucy was orphaned and came to Nick and Carol? What do you think happened to her parents?

2. When was Lucy ready to learn to fly?

3. For what reasons would Lucy have trouble living in the wild?

4. When do geese fly south (migrate) every year? Do you know why?

5. How many months after coming into Nick's and Carol's lives did Lucy leave?

6. After Lucy left, did she ever return to see Nick and Carol?

7. How many times a day did Nick and Carol fly Lucy to build up her strength? Why did they go that often?

8. What type of food did Lucy like to eat?

9. What color is a Canada goose's beak and legs?

10. What did the wildlife officials tell Nick and Carol to do with the gosling?

11. Can you house-train a goose? Why or why not.

1. May, Lucy could have hatched late, after the family left; the parents might have been killed by an animal. 2. Two months old when her feathers were long enough. 3. She was too young to survive on her own at first. Later, she didn't know who or what was a danger to her— people, dogs, other animals. 4. In the fall. They go where food is plentiful. 5. Nine months. She was shy around other geese. 6. Yes, one whole year later. 7. Twice a day – to build up her strength for fall migration. 8. Grass, dandelions, corn, and underwater plants. 9. Black. 10. They were told that wild animals belong in the wild. 11. No – their system is automatic so they cannot control when they "go".

Discussion Ideas for Parents, Teachers, & Students and Things You Can Do...

- Describe a normal Canada goose family unit. Talk about where geese live, and when, why, and how far they migrate? What are the biggest problems communities are having with the goose population? Discuss ideas on how to move geese without hurting them.

- Discuss and research the law regarding how and when to help a potentially orphaned wild animal in your area. Why do you think these laws are in place?

- Research rehabilitators in your region and state. Call them to find out their recommendations on what to do with a verified orphaned animal.

- Discuss what Nick and Carol might have done differently in the beginning with Lucy and why.

- Have a wildlife expert talk or rehabilitator talk to your group.

- Discuss the problems of human population growth and its impact on wildlife habitat.

- What does the word "ecosystem" mean? What are the different elements of an ecosystem? Why are ecosystems important and how can we protect them?

- Don't assume an animal is orphaned, and never remove an animal from the wild. Contact an expert and educate yourself.

- Volunteer with animal rescue and rehabilitation agencies.

- Donate money or time to non-profit rescue/rehabilitators.

- Check online resources at **www.RaisingLucy.com**

About the Author

Carol and her husband, Nick, raised an orphaned Canada gosling to its successful return to the wild. They didn't set out to raise a goose. In fact, at first they tried every day to find wild geese or a rehabber to help them. Because they couldn't find the help they needed they became determined to just keep the little gosling safe. As Nick and Carol raised the goose they named Lucy, they did a lot of things wrong and would never recommend that someone keep an orphaned gosling. Keeping a wild animal can lead to disastrous results. Lucy, though, transitioned successfully to the wild, but they never wanted Lucy to be a pet and are happy to know that she truly is a wild goose.

Because of the problems they had finding help, Carol is focused on supporting regional and statewide rehabilitators. Her mission is also to educate children and adults on when to help an animal—this applies to all animals. Too often an animal is separated from its parent by a well-meaning, but uninformed person. This wasn't the case with Lucy, but there are things Nick and Carol could have done differently.

The Muziks' story is true, and fortunately has a happy ending. They realize they had an ideal situation on a lake and their commitment led to the positive outcome for Lucy. They wouldn't adopt an orphaned goose again, and want to help educate others on what one should really do if this were to happen to them.

Carol's storytelling of Lucy's life through photography, video, illustration and writing, has led to teaching as an Artist in Residence through the Idaho Commission on the Arts, as well as courses in creative writing through Eastern Washington University's *Get Lit!* program. Carol's goal is to help others celebrate and connect to their regional wildlife through writing and art.

Follow Raising Lucy at www.RaisingLucy.com